63

Ways we move /
J 629.04 LAW   220336

Law, Felicia.

DATE DUE

SEP 30 '83			
OCT 25 '83			
MAR 1 '84			
FEB 18 '86			
MAR 4 '86			
NOV 12 '86			
MAY 07 '92			
MAY 1 1 '94			
AUG 14 '97			
JAN 2 8 2012			

D1473339

J   2076
629.04
LAW, FELICIA
Ways We Move

OVERSIZE

LONGLAC PUBLIC LIBRARY

First published 1980 by
Octopus Books Limited
59 Grosvenor Street
London W1

© 1980 Octopus Books Limited

ISBN 0 7064 1366 0

Produced by Mandarin Publishers Limited
22a Westland Road, Quarry Bay, Hong Kong

Printed in Hong Kong

Educational and Series advisor Felicia Law

Ways We Move

by
Felicia Law

illustrated by
Barry Rowe

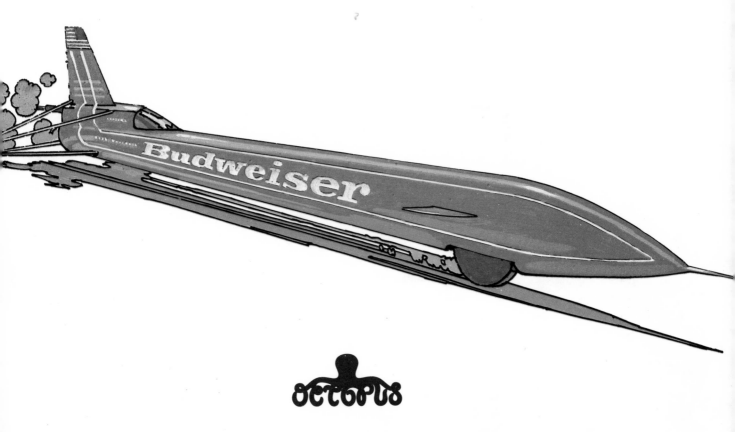

octopus

The Canoe

Canoes are small, light boats which seat one or two people who are called canoeists.

The framework of the canoe is usually made from wooden struts.

Canvas, or in the old days bark or animal skin, is stretched over the frame. Today, some canoes are made of plastic or glass-fibre.

The canoeists hold a short, flat-bladed oar called a paddle.

This is dipped into the water from side to side to propel and steer the canoe.

The Submersible

Submersibles operate in deep water carrying a small crew on an underwater exploration or on a repair mission.

Strong searchlights make it easier for the crew to see the ocean bed.

Long pincers reach out to pick up any interesting specimen that the crew want to take back to the surface.

A cable leads from the submersible to a boat on the surface. This means that people in each vessel can communicate with each other.

The Motorcycle

The motorcycle is a vehicle that runs on two wheels covered with rubber tyres.

As with a bicycle, the rider sits astride the frame and steers the motorcycle by using the handle-bars at the front.

He uses a pedal to operate the rear brake and a hand lever for the front brake.

Unlike the bicycle, the motorcycle is powered by an engine attached to the centre of its frame.

The capacity of the engine determines the power produced. It ranges from 50 cc (cubic centimetres) on lightweight cycles to as much as 1300 cc on heavyweights.

The Fighter

The fighter's main task is to destroy enemy aircraft by shooting them down.

The F-15 Eagle, shown here, is a typical moder jet fighter used by the US Airforce.

It is capable of speeds of up to 2,660 kilometres (1,650 miles) per hour.

It is a single-seat aircraft with a large amount of electronic equipment to help the pilot find and shoot down his target.

The Parachute

e parachute allows people to jump out of
craft at great heights and to float safely
wn to earth.

s a specially-designed piece of fabric that is
ked into a container on the parachutist's
k.

After he jumps the parachutist pulls a cord
which releases the parachute which then
unfolds and fills with air.

Special openings in the parachute prevent it
from swaying, so keeping the parachutist steady
when he lands. As he lands he faces into the
wind which acts as a brake. To absorb the
impact of landing he bends his knees and rolls
over gently on the ground.

The Hydrofoil

The hydrofoil travels at 148 kilometres (92 miles) per hour.

The hull is lifted above the waves on V-shaped struts attached to the bottom.

The tips of the struts are called foils and they ride through the water.

They glide at such speeds that they create 'lif just like the wings of an aircraft.

When the hydrofoil slows down, its hull retur to the water's surface like an ordinary boat.

The Hovercraft

he hovercraft skims smoothly just above the rface of the water on a cushion of air.

can go faster than vessels that have to push eir way through water.

can travel at speeds of up to 132 kilometres 0 miles) an hour when it is fully loaded.

Strong jets of air are blown under the body of the hovercraft by a very large fan.

This air streams out around the skirt at the base of the hull and lifts it above the water.

Hovercrafts are used for fast ferry services and they can travel over land as well.

The Helicopter

A helicopter is lifted into the air by powerful rotating blades.

The helicopter will turn in the same direction in which the main blade is tilted. When the main blade is horizontal, the helicopter rises.

The main rotating blade lifts the aircraft. The small blades at the tail balance the twisting force of the main blade.

The helicopter has several characteristics which make it useful in awkward places and situations.

It can land and take off vertically in small clearings, fly low over the ground, quickly change directions or hover in one sp

The Tank

Tanks are heavy fighting vehicles which can move over very rough ground on special tracks.

The crew are well protected by thick metal armour plating.

Tanks usually have a turret on the top with a large gun capable of firing shells at the enemy.

In recent wars tanks have fought each other in huge fast moving battles.

Roller Skates

Roller skates are boots with wheels attached to them.

Each boot has four wheels which contain little metal balls called bearings. These make the wheels go round smoothly.

The skater puts the skates on his feet and moves forwards, building up speed until he is wheeling across the ground.

Roller skating is great fun, but practising can be quite bumpy!

The Bicycle

The bicycle is made of two lightweight metal wheels that are covered with rubber tyres and fixed on to a strong frame.

A linked chain connects the back wheel with the pedals so that when the rider turns the pedals the back wheel rotates and the bicycle begins to move forwards.

When the brakes, attached to the handle-bars, are squeezed rubber blocks press against the wheel rims and slow the bicycle.

The rider steers the bicycle by turning the handle-bars in the direction he wants to go.

It takes a lot of practice to learn to balance

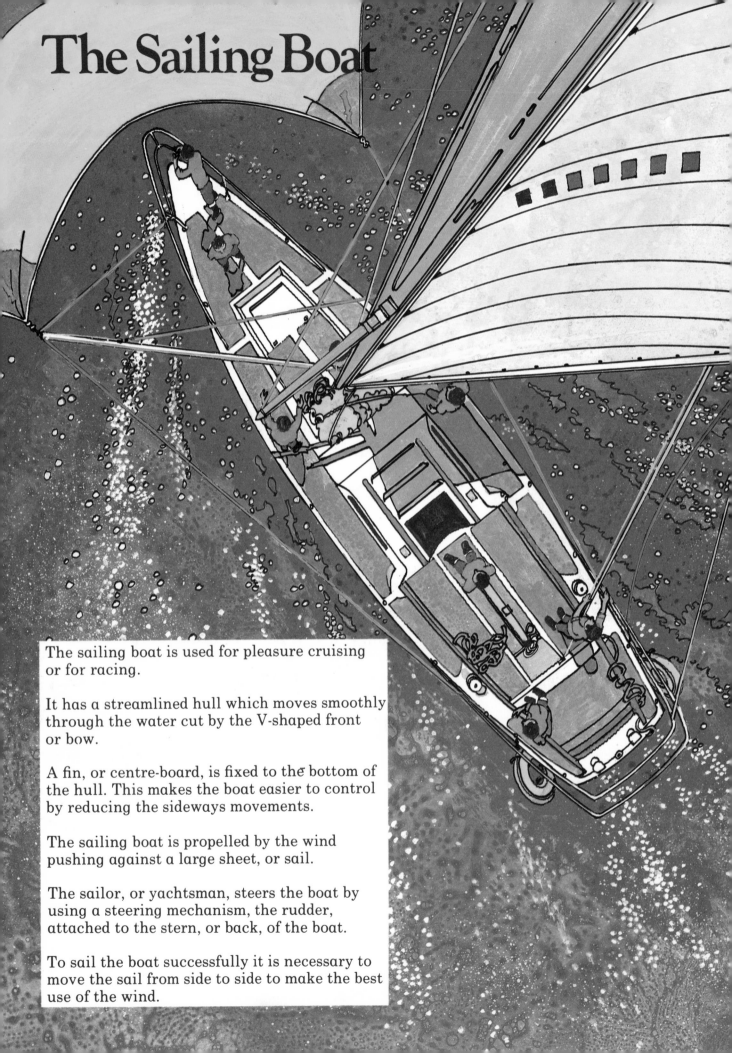

The Sailing Boat

The sailing boat is used for pleasure cruising or for racing.

It has a streamlined hull which moves smoothly through the water cut by the V-shaped front or bow.

A fin, or centre-board, is fixed to the bottom of the hull. This makes the boat easier to control by reducing the sideways movements.

The sailing boat is propelled by the wind pushing against a large sheet, or sail.

The sailor, or yachtsman, steers the boat by using a steering mechanism, the rudder, attached to the stern, or back, of the boat.

To sail the boat successfully it is necessary to move the sail from side to side to make the best use of the wind.

The Balloon

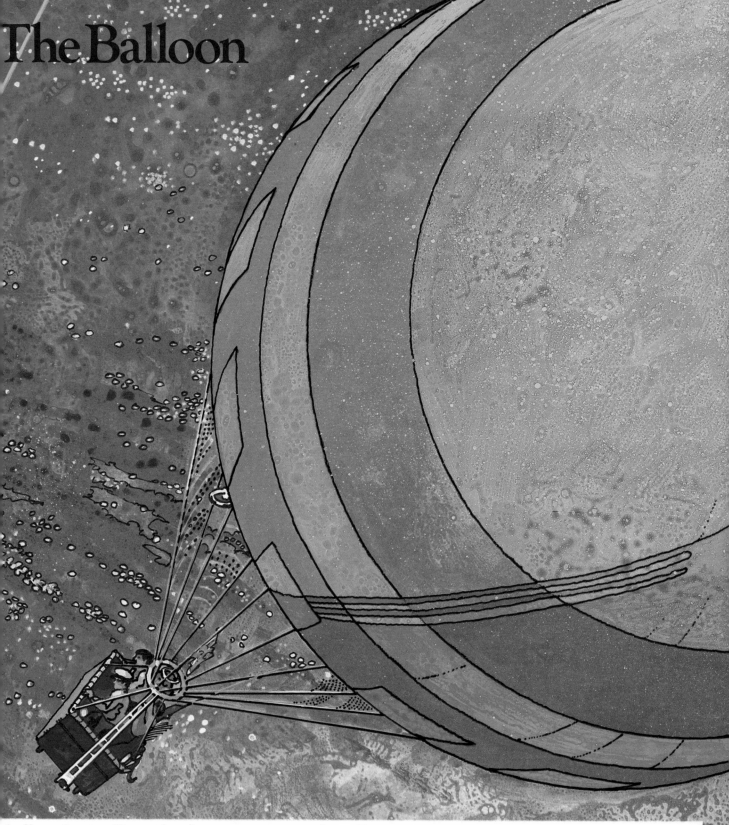

balloon is usually made of a strong man-made
aterial such as nylon.

is filled with helium gas or hot air.

he balloonist travels in a basket attached
elow the balloon.

He makes the balloon rise in the air by pumping
more gas or hot air inside. When small changes
to the balloon's altitude have to be made,
however, he empties the heavy sandbags
stored in the basket.

He makes the balloon fall by opening the neck
of the balloon and letting gas or hot air escape.

The balloon moves in the direction of the wind.

The Bobsleigh

The bobsleigh is usually manned by two or four men depending on its size.

It is made of wood or metal and is painted in bright colours.

Underneath the body are metal runners that make the 'sleigh slide down snow-covered slopes at speeds of over 144 kilometres (90 mile per hour.

The crew push it to start, running alongside it until it gathers speed and then they jump on t it. They steer it by pulling, to the right or the left, a rope connected to the front runners.

Skis

kis are worn on the feet and allow people to
avel quickly across the snow.

hey are long wooden strips that taper and
irve upwards at the front.

he underside of the skis are usually waxed to

help them run more smoothly.

The skier puts on the skis by clipping them to
specially-designed boots.

He pushes himself along and balances himself
with two sticks called poles.

The Moon Buggy

The moon buggy was designed to help the astronauts travel on the moon's surface. It is also called a Lunar Roving Vehicle (LRV).

The LRV is a compact, sturdy vehicle powered only by batteries.

It can travel over rough terrain including boulders and crevasses and climb steep slopes.

Various types of equipment used in lunar exploration are attached to the buggy and a television camera records the journey.

When samples of dust and rocks were collecte from the moon's surface during the Apollo spaceflight they were placed on the buggy's wide floor and taken back to the spacecraft.

The Jeep

jeep is used for travelling over rough ground.

has a tough suspension system to absorb
e many bumps and jolts.

most cars the engine only powers the two
ck wheels which push the car forward, but
e jeep engine gives power to all four wheels.

This gives the jeep extra grip and control.

Jeeps have a removable roof so that goods can
be loaded and unloaded easily.

The Ocean Liner

People who wish to travel across the oceans in a leisurely fashion may sail in a large passenger ship called a liner.

A liner is like a huge hotel. The passengers sleep in cabins and can meet each other in restaurants, at the swimming pool or while strolling on the decks.

Very often there are lots of shops on the ship where the passengers can buy souvenirs of their ocean voyage.

VTOL

VTOL stands for Vertical Take-Off and Landing aircraft.

This airplane can take-off and land in small clearings. It has a specially-designed engine that can either push the airplane off the ground and let it land gently on a cushion of air or, once in the air, make it fly forward like a regular airplane.

It is used by the armed services around the world because of these special characteristics

The VTOL, however, is still too small and too noisy to be used for public air transportation.

LONGLAC PUBLIC LIBRARY

Supersonic Aircraft

n airliner like the Concorde is called an SST
SuperSonic Transport.

travels faster than the speed of sound.

ound travels through the air in waves, known
s sound waves, at 330 metres (1080 ft) per
econd.

oncorde travels at more than twice the speed
sound.

hen it goes faster than the speed of sound it
uses shock waves through the air. The shock
aves cause a sonic boom. This is called
reaking the sound barrier'.

oncorde can travel over a range of 6,400
ilometres (4,000 miles) and flies at a much
igher altitude than normal jet aircrafts.

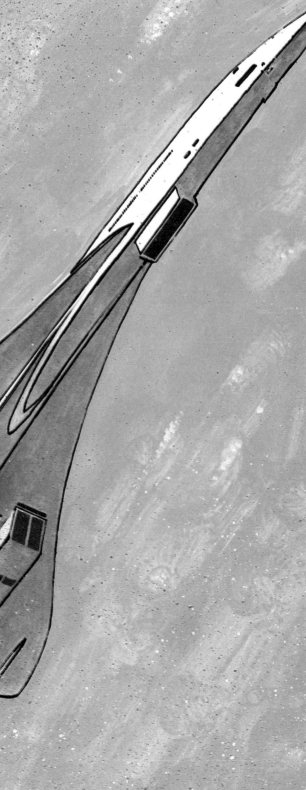

LONGLAC PUBLIC LIBRARY

The Excavator

Excavators are large tractors with a large bucket at the front.

The driver forces the bucket into the ground and scoops up huge shovelfuls of earth.

Excavators are used to clear the ground in preparation for building houses or roads.

This is an illustration of the Caterpillar 235.

The Dragster

The dragster is a very special car designed to travel extremely fast over a distance of a quarter of a mile.

It has a huge rear engine and large rear wheels with smooth tyres.

The front wheels are very small and light.

Only two cars race at a time along the driving course which is called a drag strip.

The winner is the first to reach the quarter-mile finishing post.

They are called 'funny cars' because of their unusual shape and colourful pattern.

The Cruiser

The Soviet *Kresta* Mk. II cruiser is designed for anti-submarine warfare.

It carries a helicopter which can take off and land on deck, and look out for enemy ships.

The cruiser has twin gun mounts and is equipped with radar.

Like most modern cruisers, the *Kresta* is not very large, although it is highly specialized.

The Tanker

Tankers are ships which carry oil to refineries.

Many new supertankers are extremely large and often more than 365 metres (1,200 feet) long.

The oil is held in compartments below the deck.

The engines, bridge and all the accommodation are usually situated to the rear of the tanker.

The Container Truck

A great deal of cargo is shipped around the world in huge, sealed, metal boxes called containers which protect the goods.

Containers are often carried in tiers on the decks of ships.

They are then unloaded at the docks.

Some are lifted on to the trailer of a truck an driven away to their destinations. Other containers are loaded on to trains and travel by rail.

The use of containers is a simple and safe wa of transporting goods.

The Land Speed Record Car

...pecial cars are built to break speed records
...n land.

...hey are now usually powered by jet or rocket
...ngines and use special fuels.

...n 1979, the Budweiser Rocket was driven
...cross the Bonneville Salt Flats in Utah, USA.

...reached a speed of 1,027 kilometres (638.6
...iles) per hour.

The Sand Yacht

An unusual boat with wheels races over the sand; its single sail billowing in the wind.

This is sand racing.

The vessel has a canoe-like body made of lightweight glass-fibre.

It has one sail and three wheels.

It can sometimes reach four times the wind speed and delicate manoeuvres are controlled by a steering wheel or pedals.

The Windsurfer

Wind surfing is a new type of leisure sport.

It combines the thrill of surfing with traditional sailing, using the wind to ride the waves.

The apparatus, called a windsurfer, resembles a large surfboard with a sail attached.

It is made of lightweight plastic and flexible glass-fibre.

The rider, also called a windsurfer, steers the board directly, using only his bodyweight and the different positions of the sail.

The Underground or Subway Train

This is a train powered by electricity.

It carries passengers from one part of a city to another.

The railway runs through tunnels below the surface of the ground.

Passengers reach the platform by using escalators, or moving stairs.

The Submarine

LONGLAC PUBLIC LIBRARY

The submarine is a ship that can be submerged and navigated underwater.

It has a long cigar-shaped hull made of metal which must be thick enough to support the heavy weight of water pressing down on it.

Tanks are fitted to the side of the hull. When the tanks are full of air, the submarine floats on the surface. When the tanks are full of sea water, the submarine grows heavier and sinks.

To get back to the surface, air must be blown into the tanks to push the water out again.

Submarines like the USS *Nautilus* can make long trips under the ice caps of the North Pole.

Submarines are used in warfare. and can launch rockets from under the water's surface.

The Car

The car is generally a four-wheeled vehicle powered by a petrol (gasoline) engine.

There are many different styles, colours and sizes of cars from the luxurious Rolls Royce to the tiny Ford Fiesta.

Cars are used by many people to travel to and from work or for a drive in the country.

The Train

Modern electric and diesel trains can travel very quickly.

The Japanese high speed train is called the 'Bullet' because of its shape and speed.

It is an electric engine and can travel at an amazing 210 kilometres (130 miles) per hour. It runs between Tokyo and Osaka.

It has automatic controls which make it safer and easier to drive.

Engineers all over the world are designing many new types of trains that travel on monorails, on cushions of air or are driven by electromagnetic forces.

In the future trains will be even more comfortable and faster than they are today.

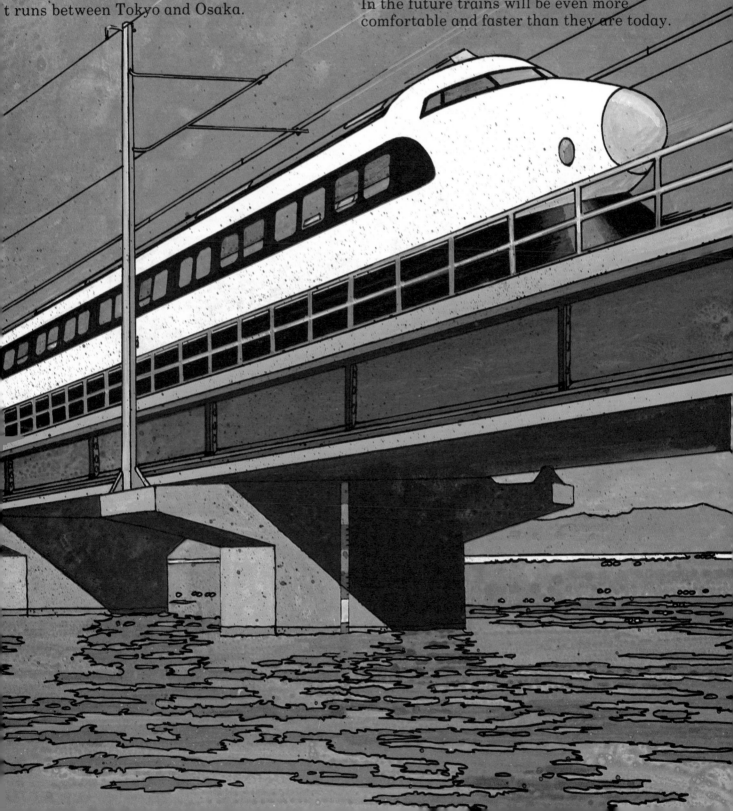

The Racing Car

Formula One racing cars are fast. They compete against one another in races all over the world, many on circuits with lots of twists and bends.

These races are called Grands Prix.

The Ferrari racing car, which was first produced in 1948 by Enzo Ferrari, has a flat twelve-cylinder engine. Ferrari cars are always painted bright red – which is the traditional racing colour of Italy. It has proved a very successful car, winning 71 Grands Prix.

The Snowmobile

Snowmobiles are motorized vehicles with one or two skis in front which help people to travel quickly and easily on the snow.

They are steered by handle-bars and by the one or two passengers shifting positions.

Some machines have been known to travel a speeds greater than 160 kilometres (100 miles per hour.

They are used for winter sport events or for winter travel and rescue missions.

The Hang-glider

ang-gliders allow men and women to float
rough the air like birds.

ang-gliders have large fixed wings which are
retched over a metal frame to resemble a
rge kite. The flier is strapped into a harness
hich hangs from this frame. He holds on to a
etal bar which is also attached to the main
ame by two struts.

To become airborne the flier quickly runs
down a steep slope, allowing the air to rush
under the kite-like wings, so lifting the hang-
glider into the air. He controls the direction of
the glider by shifting his weight along the
metal bar when in the air.

The Space Shuttle

The space shuttle acts as a ferry between space and the earth.

Like a rocket, it is launched vertically using the fuel stored in an attached, disposable tank.

When in orbit in space, it can be used as a space laboratory, a rescue vehicle or a repair station.

The most important feature of this spacecraft, however, is that it can land like an airplane and be used again and again.